Where Are You Now?

Creating a Life of Meaning and Joy by Discovering Your Balance Zone

Where Are You Now?

Creating a Life of Meaning and Joy by Discovering Your Balance Zone

Razaz Banoun

YouSpeakIt
PUBLISHING
*The Easy Way
to Get Your Book
Done Right*™

This book is dedicated to you, the person who is reading this book right now. You are the most important part of the value and success of the book because you are the one who is going to take action by applying what you read to your life, in a way that could make a difference for you, or by creating a new method that benefits you and others around you. You are a part of the Oneness that can always make our world better. Thus, I would like to thank you very much for being here at this moment and for being the motivation for me to write.

Contents

Acknowledgments

Thank you, Allah, God, for all that you have created and blessed me with in my inner and outer world. You help me enjoy my life's mission in which I changed my life and now change others' lives for the best, peacefully.

Dr. Abdullatif Banoun, I'm so happy and grateful that I am your daughter. From deep in my heart I would like to thank you for all the love, support, help, and everything I have been lucky to receive from you. You gave me the confidence and the power to start and continue many major journeys in my life successfully. This book is one of them. I love you and am so proud of writing this book with your help and encouragement. You are the hero behind this book!

I would like to say thank you to the YouSpeakIt publishing staff for translating my thoughts into a written language. My work is my language. Simply put, you have supported my belief in myself and in my actions. In helping me publish this book, you have enabled me to prove, once again, that you can do any good thing you want no matter what your spoken language is!

Introduction

In 2012, when I was learning the English language, I picked up a book called *Now Is the Time: 170 Ways to Seize the Moment* (2009), by Patrick Lindsay. The book had short sentences and examples, and it functioned as an excellent base for me to start learning the language.

I found this quotation, attributed to Winston Churchill, in Patrick Lindsay's book:

Attitude is a little thing that makes a big difference.

When I read this sentence for the first time, I remember feeling so happy that I could understand this simple but profound sentence—in English!

The concept of *attitude* was intriguing to me, so I put some more thought into it.

What is the best definition of the word?

What did it mean to me?

How would I explain it to somebody else?

A lot of people think that *attitude* describes something immense, something you have deep within you that has taken many years to develop.

From my point of view, however, *attitude* is best defined in the context of the moment. Attitude can be described as *the consciousness of the moment,* in which you are aware of what you are doing, what you are feeling, and what you are thinking about in that moment.

To enjoy your life, and to enjoy the moment in which you are living, all that you need is a conscious attitude. This kind of consciousness will give you an awareness of ideas and feelings and an ability to appreciate fully the meaning of the moment.

It is your attitude that enables you to recognize the importance of taking action, changing something, doing something — or perhaps ceasing to do something — in your life. In each moment, our attitudes are key to finding balance in our lives.

I understood this before I started to learn the English language, but it was later, after being here in the United States, that I began to delve deeper into this concept.

I began to ask these related questions:

- How does attitude impact balance in my life?
- How can I find balance in my relationships?
- How do I find balance within myself?
- How can I understand myself, and how can I understand other people better?

- How can I best interpret the meaning of the situations I am in?

I found myself writing notes in my journal about how to find balance, and how to live in the moment—as well as how to discern whether I was in the moment or not. Finally, those notes evolved into the writing of the book you hold in your hand.

This book was written to help you find your own *balance zone,* and to learn how to use that zone to convert ideas into real action. The balance zone is that space in which you can feel that you have everything. In this zone, you exist in the awareness of the moment. You can be happy, no matter what. You can develop balanced relationships with others, with yourself, and with the situations of your life.

I wrote down my thoughts and experiences for you in the hope that they will make a difference in your life, that they will help you to find balance, and to find the joy of living a balanced life.

This book can be read in a very short time, but it requires more time for you to go deeper, to reach what's beyond the words. You may read more into what was written, and you may see something different in my words than what I meant. That is to be expected because we are a community of unique people, each with our own unique perceptions of the moment.

I confidently recommend to you that you read this book at least twice. The first time, read it very fast. The second time, however, read it at your leisure. Read it a little at a time or dive into a particular chapter and live in it for a while.

If you'd like to read the book for a second or third time, imagine that you are going to read a new book you have never read before — it's not a coincidence that you feel like reading it again. Maybe a message is there for you, or perhaps, an inspiration. Be conscious as you read. Whatever value you find in this book will take root and continue from your consciousness.

Of course, it's easy to say something — and it's easy to read it — but sometimes it takes a little bit of effort to apply it. To make changes in your life will require some work.

What areas of your life are in need of change?

You may want to work on one of these areas:

- Your relationships with others
- Your relationship with yourself
- Understanding love
- Attitude toward money
- Living in the moment
- Being aware and conscious of the importance of the moment

Each of these areas is discussed in this book, and I have worked on all of them in my own life. In some areas, I feel that I have reached a very high level. In other areas — for example, my relationship with money — I've had more difficulty, and I'm still working, using the ideas I have written about.

In reality, life is a journey of development. When I work on applying changes in my life, I think of it as developing or expanding my consciousness. The important thing to realize is that this kind of endeavor never ends. We all have work to do. If you already have reached a high level in an area of development, okay. Now is your time to go even higher, to enjoy even more, to go deeper into whatever area you want.

My hope for you is that you learn to expand your consciousness more and more, using all of your experiences, using everything you enjoy and absorb along the way. I hope that this book can help you on your journey.

You can make great changes in your life. You can find a life of balance, meaning, and above all, joy.

CHAPTER ONE

Time

WHERE ARE YOU NOW?

Imagine you are a tightrope walker.

What is the first thing you want to do before you start your walk?

You'll want to look around you so you know where you are. You can see what the conditions are and take note of any dangers. Then, place your feet on the exact point where you will start your walk. Center yourself here by becoming aware of your breath and fully conscious of your balance. This is the same approach you should have when you meet any challenge.

Be Aware of Everything around You

Where are you right now?

Give yourself a moment to look around you and notice:

- Where are you sitting?
- Are you reading a paper book or an electronic book?

- What clothing are you wearing?
- What is the scent of the room?
- Where are you in this moment?

I often ask on social media: *Where are you now?*

This simple question induces all kinds of answers — real, metaphorical, physical, and non-physical. Some people immediately think about their present geographical location and might say they are in a specific city or country. Others think about the place of their current activity, such as a wonderful restaurant, college, work, or home. Many talk about what they are doing or what they are learning. Some might focus on how they are feeling at that moment.

The question makes people pay more attention to their feelings, thoughts, and surroundings. It has created a powerful connection between my followers and me, especially on Snapchat, where they enjoy sharing an immediate picture with me to answer the question. In asking the question, I think I call them back to the present moment when they have lost awareness of it. My goal is to help them be present in each moment in any way that helps shift their level of awareness.

It is your turn to ask yourself the question. Observe the elements around you — what you are doing, thinking, and feeling. Become aware of yourself. Become aware of what is around you.

Where You Are: Location, Day, and Time

When you become aware of everything around you, it will help you see, with more clarity, what's going on around you. It can help you come to a better understanding of what time is, what life is, and what you are.

Let's begin with the concept of time. There are two different aspects to consider.

The first is factual: This tells you the actual time and date in your location. For example, you might be in the city of Montreal, and it is 2:30 p.m. on the nineteenth of June. These are facts that apply to you, as well as to everyone else in the city.

The second is subjective, and it applies only to you.

Consider where you are right now — your location, the day and the time.

When you think about the time, think about your time of life. You have a past and a future, but you are existing in a particular time of your life right now. When you think about location, think about where you are in the progress of your life. You are in a certain place right now, and that place is unique to your life.

Here are some specific questions to ask yourself:

- *What is that time like?*

- *What is that place like?*
- *Am I okay? How do I feel at this time?*
- *Am I happy, or am I feeling sad?*
- *Am I feeling disappointed or encouraged?*
- *What does this time mean to me?*
- *What does this day mean to me?*
- *Is it just a day like every day?*
- *What are my desires at this place and time of my life?*
- *Do I want to have something different than I have?*
- *Am I trying to achieve something?*
- *Am I looking for something – perhaps joy, peace, or love?*

Every day is a different day, and each time and place has its own character, challenges, and joys. Each has a different meaning for every person.

Are You Holding the Past or the Future with You at This Moment?

Time can be thought of as divided into past, present, and future – if we use a physical definition. Time is a way of measuring what exists between moments. For me, however, the meaning of time is *now*.

From my point of view, therefore, time actually has no time. It can't be measured. It is an instantaneous moment. It is *now*.

Think about it. Take a moment to meditate on this idea:

- *Am I held in the past?*
- *Am I running after the future?*
- *Do I feel alive in this moment?*

Consider the idea that there is no time — no past, no future. There is only now. Meditate on your breathing.

Are you breathing in the past?

No.

Are you breathing in the future?

No.

You are just breathing *now*.

If you understand this, you can understand the principle of *time as now*.

Now, let's ask the initial question again from this new perspective: Where are you now?

Do you hold the past or future with you at this moment?

If you are living with emotional burdens, it may be because you are holding on to the past. In this case, you will have difficulty focusing on the moment in front of you. Conversely, if you are always fretting and worrying about what might happen, you are fixed on the future, making it impossible to enjoy the moment.

Instead, can you deal with the issues of the moment, then put them away to enjoy the new moment?

Can you make your plans for the future, then put them away and come back to enjoy a new moment?

If you can, then, in this moment, your hands won't always be filled with the future or the past. This makes your hands available to hold the moment. This is what I mean.

I want to go back to the example of the tightrope walker. Imagine that you are that person. You are ready to step off the platform.

Considering everything we've discussed, can you answer the question: *Where am I now?*

Are you truly in the moment?

Are you truly ready to take a step forward?

If you aren't ready, think about what you need to do to make yourself ready to take that step forward.

WHERE DO YOU WANT TO BE?

Your life is entirely your responsibility. Consciously or subconsciously, you have made a decision to take yourself somewhere, and that is where you are. Life is a journey. We move through our lives, from station to station, and you are responsible for every stop along the way. You arrive where you choose to arrive.

You might be thinking: *That doesn't make sense. I don't like where I am. Why would I choose to be here?*

It is true that sometimes we choose, subconsciously, to arrive in a place we don't like at all. Nonetheless, we are responsible for our choices, and there is a reason we have arrived where we are.

Accept responsibility for your choices. Moving forward in your life depends on it.

Past Is Past Unless You Keep It

As I mentioned earlier, time consists only of now.

If this is true, what is the past?

The past is something that has already passed, which means it is behind you. It's already gone. Whether you are speaking literally or figuratively, the past is not here anymore. However, you can keep it alive if you are actively keeping it with you.

It's true that you can't keep it physically. You can't hold it in your hand—it isn't like an object you can hold. However, as long as you are focused on what happened in the past, you can't move forward. As long as you are fixated on what caused you to do something, or on what has been done to you, you will never be ready to start this moment — and, if you can't start this moment, nothing can change.

The Future Escapes if You Run After It

What is the future?

The future is ahead of us. It hasn't happened yet. The future is *always* ahead of us, and it escapes if you run after it. If you are focused on what you want in the future, or what you fear in the future, you will be spending your energy thinking about something that is always out of your reach.

- *Am I going to get that?*
- *Am I going to accomplish that?*
- *Is this going to happen?*

If you are mentally attached to the future, you will never feel certain about anything. You will always feel that there is something escaping from you, because you are trying to catch it.

Try to recall a time when you wanted something so badly that you were consumed with wanting. All your energy was focused on wanting, wanting, wanting. Then, after receiving it, you looked back and regretted that you missed a lot of fun and happiness by focusing on what you were waiting for rather than enjoying what you already had.

Perhaps when you reach that goal, you might feel a surprising lack of happiness about it. Sometimes, by the time you receive what you wanted, other factors have arisen that make you feel that you no longer really need what you had been waiting for. It doesn't give you any joy or happiness anymore.

Sometimes you may keep running after something but never get it. Usually, it's not because it's so hard to get; it's because you are consumed with the need itself. As long as you have that need, you will simply keep running into the future after that goal.

Although you may not ever get it, you will forever run toward the future in this fashion, saying to yourself repeatedly: *I don't have this, and I want it.*

> *We must let go of the life we have planned,*
> *so as to accept the one that is waiting for us.*
> ~ Joseph Campbell

No matter what your plan, you can choose to either run after the future or be willing to receive what you want — what is coming to you — by practicing patience, belief, and conscious living in the moment! You don't need to run toward the future, but you need to learn how to be a better receiver, opening doors for the things you want to come into your life. Consciousness and awareness are the ways to accomplish this.

Between Falling Down and Being Stuck

Visualize yourself as the tightrope walker in the beginning of this chapter. Imagine that you are off-balance while you are walking this journey.

There are two potential consequences. First, if you lose your balance, you may fall down. Second, if you become consumed with trying to keep your balance so that you won't fall, you won't be able to move forward. You will be stuck where you are, in the middle of the rope.

Let's look at how this scenario relates to our discussion of past and future. Tightrope walkers carry a balancing stick. Imagine that you are walking along the rope, holding your balancing stick out. Your balancing stick is composed of two equal parts. On one side is the past; on the other is the future.

You try to walk across the tightrope, but you are having a hard time staying balanced. It could be that the past is weighing you down on one side, or the future is weighing you down on the other. Either way, as you try to walk forward, you will fall.

You may be able to hold your body in a way to offset the balance stick, but you must remain frozen in this position. If you step forward, you will fall.

Similarly, when you are weighed down by the past or the future, you can't keep yourself balanced. You can't focus on the moment. Unfortunately, a focus on the moment is exactly what is required to walk the tightrope.

You must say to yourself: *Okay, the only time I have is now, and I am going to walk forward, ignoring what's on the right or left. I must focus and give all my inertia to this point, then move on without letting fear hold me back.*

This is the only way you can empower yourself to walk forward, without falling down or getting stuck.

When you feel that you don't know where you are, or you don't know where you want to be, give yourself a moment. Remember that the past is past, which means it's gone. Remember that the future is far away from you, and it's going to escape from you if you run after it.

Take a deep breath and say: *Okay, I am here in this moment, and this is where I want to be. I want to be here, not holding something that is gone, and not running after something that hasn't been yet.*

FIND YOUR SELF-TRUTH

Who are you?

It is a common question. When you start a new job, join a new group, or meet a new person, you might be asked this question.

What does it mean when someone asks you who you are?

Usually, they want to know your name, and perhaps what your job or position is.

I would guess—because you are reading this book—that you have asked yourself the question as well.

Who am I?

In either case, no matter who is asking the question, the answer is complex. It involves both *facts*—what everyone knows about you, and *truth*—your deep internal identity.

Who You Are: Facts and Truth

First, let's deal with the facts.

Who you are, in fact, consists of items like:

- Your name and other identifying information
- Where you are now

- Where you have been
- Where you work
- What you have accomplished
- How old you are

Anyone may know these facts about you.

In contrast, what I call the *self-truth*—the truth that is related to you being on this unique life journey—may not be obvious. You may have discovered some parts of it. You may have known some of it for a while. As long as you are breathing and you are alive, however, you will always be realizing more of your self-truths.

This self-truth is an identity that is formed by a combination of:

- Consciousness
- Beliefs
- Feelings
- Thoughts
- Experiences
- Self-esteem
- Self-worth
- Self-confidence

Your self-truth is the place where you are sitting now. You may not always be expressing all of it to others, but this truth is in you. It is a part of you. You can go to this truth to ask questions and receive answers, but you must take care that you ask the questions in the context of the moment.

For example, imagine you go within—to your self-truth—and you ask yourself: *Where am I?*

Pay attention to your internal response. You may immediately think or feel something from the past, or a thought about the future might come to mind right away. Be aware that these cannot be from your self-truth. Self-truth is not in the past and it's not in the future.

If you have spent all of your days thinking about the future, and you think of your self-truth in terms of what you are going to have in the future—this is not your self-truth, it is your *self-expectation.*

If you ask a question and find yourself immersed in the past, and see your self-truth in terms of what happened in the past—this is not your self-truth, it is your *self-communication.*

Your authentic self-truth will say, "Here's where you are *now."*

Between Your Choices

When you let yourself go deeply inward so you can make that connection between you and your self-truth, you are going to find that you have unlimited options.

You have unlimited choices. Self-truth, as I've said, is a combination of everything that has made you who you are now.

At every crossroads of your life, you have choices. In your life, you have made innumerable choices already. In other words, you live your life on a road that offers choices constantly.

For example, imagine you are trying to find your self-truth in this moment. You ask the question while you are envisioning both the past and future as important elements in your life. You have many choices. One choice, for example, is keeping what you have from the past, and considering it 100 percent your self-truth. There is no way for you to feel better than what you have felt even a minute ago.

It's true that your past has played a huge part in your life. What happened in the past — your experience, your emotion, your belief — has hugely impacted your facts or self image. That's all true, but it's only part of the story. It's not your self-truth.

Instead of defining your truth by what happened in your past, you can choose to say: *Okay, I am living in this moment, with gratitude for everything that I have had, and with the intention of being open to receive any assistance — feelings, support, positive energy, or something else — that can help me to make my life better.* These gifts might come to you from outside or even from your inner voice.

This choice will enable you to enjoy a new version of you in this moment. Even if you don't know it, you can make a great thing better.

On the other hand, if you are sitting in this moment— let's say you are reading this book—and you say: *Oh, what this book can do for my personality! I can be a different person in the future!*

In this case, you are moving toward a choice that won't help you right now in this moment. Instead, you can just feel the self-truth within you. All that you need now is to be present, grateful for whatever you have had in the past and grateful for whatever you may have coming in the future.

You Can't Live in Two Times at Once

Imagine you are seeking self-truth, as we were talking about in the last section. When you are searching for understanding and insight, you will be presented with a lot of choices, as we've discussed.

If you are not living in the moment, let's consider some of the other possibilities:

- You could be in this moment and, emotionally, be immersed in the past.

- You could be in this moment while you worry about the future.

- You could be in the moment, thinking about the past, and worrying about the future at the same time.

- You could be thinking about the past and future, and not be in the moment at all.

Ask yourself: *Where is the truth? When you look at each of these options and these forces that pull between opposite sides, what is the truth?*

For example, is it true that you can live in the present moment while you are emotionally affected by the past?

Some might say, confidently, "Oh, I am living in the moment, while I am still thinking about the past."

Honestly, you can't be that way, although some people will always say that they can. The fact is—you can't live in two times at once. Although it may seem like you can exist in the present while you are occupied by the past, this is an illusion.

In each minute, you can be in only one time-space. If you are torn between the past and the present, perhaps in the first half of a minute, you are affected by the past, and then, in the second half of the minute, you may catch yourself and come into the present, but you can't live in both times at once. You may think you are living both, but the truth is that you are not.

You Are the Truth

So what is the truth?

What is the truth among all these elements, all these unlimited choices, all these potentials you are living in this moment?

From my point of view, the answer is this:

You are the truth.

You are the only truth that has existed in this moment, because everything around you only exists because *you* exist. All the facts surrounding you, all the truths that belong to you — without you, none of it would exist at all in this moment.

Meditate on this idea. My hope is that you can enjoy finding your own self-truths each day. Enjoy exploring yourself. A new version of you may be found in every single moment, even if you are doing nothing but existing silently in peace and love.

It may seem like those quiet moments are unimportant, but even when you aren't doing anything, or thinking deep thoughts, you are living a unique moment. Believe me, in any moment, you will always be able to find a new self-truth growing inside of you if you look for it. Don't focus on all the facts and timelines, but look at yourself as the truth in this moment, and enjoy.

Treasure this journey. Rejoice in it like a kid who has a new toy, like a LEGO piece. Imagine you have a new LEGO piece, and you are trying to figure out what you can create or what you can discover with that new piece. Think about how it may combine with the pieces you already know and love. Enjoy the process of seeing something new.

Try not to take everything too seriously, but instead, take it in with the joy of living, and find your self-truth every day. Give yourself permission to feel the joy of life. In any moment—for example, this one—you can stop and do nothing but be aware of your breathing for a minute, without saying anything, and just enjoy what you feel about yourself. Believe, and be grateful for the truths that you find.

Imagine yourself as the tightrope walker once again. Know that it is possible for you to move peacefully and happily, and, at the same time, be completely focused on what you are doing. Remember that in order to move, you must stand up in the zone where there is no time but now. You can't keep your balance while you are carrying burdens from the past or the future.

Are you feeling pushed down by the past?

Are you feeling pulled into the future?

In moments when your balance is in jeopardy, take a deep breath and remind yourself that there is a zone — let's call it the *zero* zone — where you can stand in perfect balance. From here, you can walk forward toward your goals with confidence.

CHAPTER TWO

Love

DO YOU REALLY NEED LOVE?

Wherever I travel, I can find a poster or painting that states:

ALL YOU NEED IS LOVE

It's always a bit different from one space to another, from one city to another. There are different designs, sometimes in amazing colors. The artwork is designed, of course, to attract the passerby to buy it.

Every time I read these words, they inspire a question: *Do you really need love?*

For many years, there were times when I really didn't have any answer for that question. I'd just keep asking myself: *Do I really need love?* And I couldn't answer the question.

Imagine you see a sign with that beautiful quote.

Would you buy it?

Just think about it: Is it true that all you need is love?

Have You Found Love?

Have you found love in your life?

Answering this question can be very easy for some of you. For others, it may be very difficult. Maybe you have already have found your answer, but maybe you are the way I used to be. I was trying so hard to find love. It was like shopping, searching everywhere for something I wanted. I looked for it in things, in others, in the moment, and in adventures. Finally, I figured out where it was already going on — in my life.

Personally, after years and years of exploring who I am and why I'm here, I can say that it's not easy to find love, but it's not hard, either.

The Truth of Love

To find the answer to all questions, look for the *truth of love*.

If you simply knew where you could find this truth, then you would not need to go anywhere else for your answers.

The truth of love is simply that love is always here. Love has always existed in you. Love is always connected to you. Love doesn't need to be found. Love needs you just to be aware of it. Love needs you to pay attention to what's inside of you and make that connection between you and your truth.

The truth of love is the truth of you. When you are in balance, in that quiet moment when you can go deeply inside, you can start to enjoy it, start to release it, start to let the love show up and express *you,* through what you have inside of you.

The Source of Love

Since the truth of love exists inside of you, the source of love is *you.*

Do you understand this?

It can be very hard to see. For some people, I'm sure it is clear. Others may feel it to some extent, but not fully. Still others may understand at some times, but their understanding is fleeting; they don't feel it all the time.

You are the source of love.

Once you can accept this, it may take some time to get to the point where you really, completely feel and experience this phenomenon.

No matter where you are on this scale of understanding, your strategy is the same. Try to look at the things around you that you really love—deeply love—and when you immerse yourself in this feeling, you can start to get the idea. In these specific areas, you will feel that you are the source of love.

For example, if you are a mom, just look at the feelings you have for your kids. That is love, and you are the source of that love. When you are giving love like this, it means you are the source of love. It originates with you. You experience this love first before you give it to others. That's all you need to learn how to love more. Experience more inside of you, and then you can give more.

For another example, you may be working at a job and be successful at it. You may be giving your work an energy that might be love; you might love what you do. So, you are giving love; it's not work. It's not physical—it's love. You are the source of that love.

Do you feel like you are in need of love?

No matter what situation you are in—whether you are a mom or dad, husband or wife, a student or a career professional—if you feel you need love, maybe that's because you are kind of lost. Maybe you aren't paying attention to the truth that *you* are the source of love.

TIME AND LOVE

Let's go back to the example of the tightrope walker. Look at yourself, taking into account time and love together. Imagine that you are the tightrope walker, and you are ready to walk.

What should you consider most: time, or the feelings you have?

You Don't Need to Love the Past

We've already talked about time, and you know that when you walk on this tightrope, if you are attached to the past or the future, you won't be able to continue. You will either fall, or you will be forced to stand still.

Now, how does love enter into the journey?

Many people love their past more than they love the moment. Some may fall so in love with their past that it changes the way they experience life.

Time is only now. Time is this moment.

If you are in love with your past—for whatever things happened then, for any love stories you have had in your life—you will constantly find yourself visiting there to feel that love. That love, however, does not exist in the present; that romance you had was in the past. If you stay there, you can never let the love inside of you experience the moment that is happening now.

You don't need to love your past—but this doesn't mean you can't be grateful for the past. You can have gratitude for what you've had in your past, but you don't need to love it *because you already have.* You can remember and appreciate that past love, but you must keep it in the past so you can share your love with this moment.

This moment is the only moment in which you can release your love and let it splash everywhere, in all directions, to enjoy now and later, or to move on.

Who Deserves to Be Loved Now?

Whenever I think about a beautiful memory or a lovely moment I have had in the past, I enjoy the memory so much that I might think thoughts like these:

Oh, I wish that memory would stay!

I wish I could recall that moment back into existence.

I wish I were like that now.

Do you ever feel this way?

I'm sure many people do. It is okay to have these thoughts, but we can find a way to bring ourselves back to the present. If you can be grateful for what you had in the past, and understand that the past is past, you can use that experience to bring yourself fully into the current moment, to the now, with love.

You can have your balance in this moment, and live in this powerful space and time, but you must bring yourself to this awareness.

How do you find this awareness?

I ask myself this question: *Who deserves to be loved now?*

Try it now. Ask yourself this question and give yourself a few seconds to answer. Disregard the past and the future when you are thinking about it. Consider only this moment.

In this moment, who deserves to be loved?

When I ask myself, I find myself answering first: *I deserve to be loved.*

After that, I find many, many other parts of my life that deserve to be loved in this moment. My daughters, my son, my husband, my family, and my parents all deserve to be loved in this moment. My job, all that I do in my life, the people I'm helping, the bird I see flying in the sky, the very ground I'm walking on—these all deserve to be loved, right now, in this moment.

In your life, who deserves to be loved right now?

When you answer this question, envision each element of your life that deserves to be loved, in this moment. It will help you to feel the joy of loving in the moment, and so, it will bring you into the moment.

How Long Should You Love?

We sometimes put a great deal of focus on the length of time we do something.

When you succeed in getting back to this moment and you feel the love of the moment, and the joy of spreading your love, and sending that energy out to the world, it may not be long before you start to worry: *How long can this last? How long should I love?*

Be aware that these questions set you off your balance because they tilt you out of the moment and into the future. You may wonder what you will be asked to do in the future, and you may worry if you will be able to do it.

I sometimes find myself asking myself these questions:

How can I always feel good?

How can I always stay in touch with the love inside of me?

How can I continue to let it come out and sing to all people?

Getting sidetracked by these questions about the future will only cause pressure and a feeling of being out of control and out of balance.

Here it is important to regain your awareness and tell yourself: *I am in this moment. I'm not even a minute late.*

Try to pull yourself back to the moment to regain a state of balance that makes you feel right. Find the strength to resume enjoying this moment and what you are feeling right now, exactly like the person who is standing on the tightrope and wants to walk.

You don't need to think about how long you should feel a certain way, or how long you will stay in this state of readiness to experience love and express love. Just love in this moment. Loving this moment, sending love to all the people you love, and to everything around you, is enough.

If you are pulled out of balance by your worries about time and love, return to your silent zone and regain your balance. Remind yourself that what deserves to be loved now is you, as well as everything in your life. Send love out, and enjoy this moment of light that comes from inside of you.

LOVE IS LOVE

As I mentioned earlier, you are the source of love, and the truth of love is your truth. It is inside of you at this very moment. In spite of this, you may find yourself asking what love is. That's what happened to me for many years. I was always trying to find a definition for love. I tried to find the answer by reading and listening to people, and sometimes, simply meditating by myself. For years, no matter how I searched, I could not find a definition of love that satisfied me.

Love Is Undefinable

As I searched, I noticed that different people have different definitions of love.

Some of these different ideas are listed below:

- Some think that love is an appreciation for what you have.

- Others describe it as being in true harmony with someone or something.

- For some, love means the absence of fear.

- For kids, love might be playing or sharing time with other kids.

- Love can be seen as a connection to others, a physical or emotional connection.

- Love can be described as the care that we receive from others.

- Love can be defined as the nurturing we provide for our children, grandchildren, and other family members.

Because there are so many different definitions, and your definition can change, I have come to this conclusion: *Love is undefinable.*

If you do define it for yourself, your definition will be based on what you feel now in this moment, or what you are aware of in this moment, but maybe only a moment later, you could have another definition. So don't try to find a definition for it. It isn't necessary to define love in order to experience it.

Reflect Love

Whatever potential you have in your life, if you are in the state of trying to define love, you can observe the direction of love, and you can be the reflection for love.

Start by simply observing or noticing the things around you. Identify what attracts you. Whatever is attracting you is connected to something inside of you. Identify your feelings about love; your feelings reflect what is inside of you.

The scholars who research human development speak about the role of reflections in your life and how these mirrors can help you to know more about yourself. It helps to know what you like and what you don't like. It helps you to know what vibrations you are connected to.

Imagine you are single, and you have had a bad love experience — or a couple of bad experiences. Even so, whenever you see any couple full of love and happiness, you immediately feel that love and happiness inside of you. You feel happy for them, and you are happy that you are seeing them.

Remember that this is a reflection of what you have inside of you — what you feel and what you love. It shows you that you love a happy relationship, a successful relationship. That's why you noticed it; that's why you were on the same vibration with it. You already loved it deep inside of you, without thinking about it. You didn't need to define love to feel this. Because it is inside you, it's reflecting outward naturally.

Whenever you feel some kind of ego inside you that is insisting that you define love, say to yourself: *I don't need to define love, because I am reflecting love whenever I am giving to people or whenever I am spreading this energy. I don't need to define love because I am the source of love, and I am enjoying love in everything around me.*

Surrender to Love

When you focus on your need to know what love is or on seeking love from others, you pull farther away from the sources of love. When your ego drives you to define, to prove, or to know, you are losing love and balance — consciously or subconsciously.

If you find yourself making statements of knowledge like the ones listed below, it is likely you are being pulled off balance:

I know the source of love.

I have love, and I can do anything.

Now, I am sure I know the definition of love.

Be kind to yourself while you are on this journey. Give yourself permission to experience love on different levels of consciousness. Choose a time in your day or week to relax and expand your awareness of love. Then, enjoy your progress in knowing and realizing what love can be.

You need to surrender to love and simply feel it. Afterward, you can realize and experience what love looks like, inside of you, in your inner world. You will believe that love is undefinable, and you can simply reflect love and notice the reflection of love in your life, without any words, without any definition. If you are not at this point yet, just remind yourself that what you need is to surrender to love.

This surrendering is what will make you happy. To be inside the zone is to be in a state of surrender to love, which means surrendering to what you have inside of you right now. You don't need anything else.

When you surrender to something, it means that you have broken through all resistance. When there is no resistance between you and what you have surrendered to, you will find you have a great new connection between you and the world inside of you, to the love that has existed inside of you since you were born.

You can read a lot about the definition of love. It's good to know what others are thinking. It can be amazing to discover different concepts from different people. It's also important to be observant in your life and to identify what the reflection of love is in your life, in order to improve your connection with the love inside of you.

Try, as much as you can to surrender to love and to connect to your inner world; but, if you are having trouble with this, just relax and enjoy this statement:

Love is love.

Simply take yourself back to that zone — the zero zone, the balance zone — where you can feel this truth and say: *Love is love. Let me enjoy the depth of this meaning and experience this in my life. Let me experience this with my soul, with my spirit — not with my mind or my ego.*

You can't live happily and reach peace in your life without love, but, at the same time, you don't really need love because love already exists inside of you. So if you are still trying to find love — stop. Stop going from one place to another, and look at what you already have inside you.

To help yourself, just ask: *How could I be the source of love?*

But don't answer this question. Don't ponder on it. Just allow it to focus your attention on the truth that is inside of you in this moment.

This question doesn't need to be *answered,* although it needs to be *asked.*

Whenever you find yourself at a point where you feel lost between something in the past or dreams of the future, always pull yourself back to your center, to your balance zone, where you feel that this moment is the time you have now and that here is where you really can experience love.

Remember, this minute is the only minute in which you can send love, experience love, and splash your love all over—to the universe, to all the people around you, to everything in your life.

Don't forget that you are always the first one who deserves to be loved in this moment now. Bring yourself back to this zone and this balance where you can enjoy your life more and more—without ever finding a definition for love—just by surrendering to love and feeling that love is love. Love is existing in you.

CHAPTER THREE

Self-Confidence

YOU AND OTHERS ON THE SCALE

For many years, I have observed the way that people in social groups behave with each other. I have noticed that, in any group—business or personal, friends or family—people always seem to be trying to judge themselves and each other.

Consciously or subconsciously, people in a group tend to try to:

- Justify their actions
- Compare themselves to each other or the group
- Defend or apologize for their personality quirks
- Explain any differences that exist between people
- Prove that others are better than them
- Prove that they are better than others

Most of the time—99 percent of the time—you will find yourself in social situations in which you or others are looking at people around you, making these kinds of judgments. We create scales that we use to compare ourselves with each other. It's all about up and down, better or worse, bigger or smaller, or a combination of these comparisons.

Consider these questions:

- Do you think that we have to have these scales?

- Do we constantly have to think about how we compare to others?

- Why do we always have to judge ourselves and others?

- Do you think our relationships should be assessed on these scales?

Measuring Yourself

As a little girl, I used to measure myself based on the adults I admired, or whether I was doing well in school, or if I had been a great little girl, behaving well and having a good attitude.

When I became an adult, the type of measuring changed for me, but it still had the same idea or direction, consciously or subconsciously.

It is a way of thinking: *I always have to measure myself to see how I am and to see how we are, to judge this behavior, this attitude, this skill.*

We want to know: *Am I good or bad?*

Most of us — at least all through childhood — were in this same situation, in which we constantly measured ourselves against some scale. We felt pushed to keep measuring ourselves, as well as others, until a certain age of our lives: until the time we started being conscious, ready for who we are.

Sometimes, you may find that you actually love to measure yourself because it's kind of satisfying to your ego, your parents, or your friends. We are comfortable with this practice because it's been part of our lives since we were kids. We have been raised to follow the rules, to think about what others say about us, and how others look at us. There are people who cannot stop this; they continue measuring themselves until they die.

However, some reach the point in their lives where they stop and say to themselves: *Hey, stop measuring me!*

Can you stop measuring yourself and just enjoy being who you are?

Do you really feel that measuring yourself is what makes you strive to be better?

Does measuring yourself help you to be lighter or more conscious?

Consider what your answer is now, and then answer it again when you reach the end of this chapter.

Classifying Others

We tend to classify people who come into our lives. When it comes to our relationships, friends we have known, colleagues we just started working with, or any new people who come into our lives, subconsciously we find ourselves compelled to classify people. We also want to classify every situation, job, or event in our lives. It's just our nature as human beings. We want to know what this new thing is, exactly. We want to know what we can call it so we can deal with it in a way that makes sense.

We routinely classify people. We need to label them with words that put them in a certain category.

Why do we always do this?

Is it necessary?

In the workplace, classification is sometimes part of the job. We may need to classify a person as, say, someone who works days and has a particular designation or certification. However, there are many occasions when the classifying of people is completely unnecessary, yet we do it anyway. We do it routinely. Considering these issues prompted me to meditate a little bit more on the subject.

How do we classify people on a daily basis?

We use words to describe where they fall on a scale, or words that compare them with ourselves or others.

We say things like:

- *Abby is cute, but Ellen is beautiful.*
- *My daughter is a genius.*
- *Ahmad is not as confident as Sarah.*
- *My friend's son is a quiet boy, not like his brother.*

We do this every day, whether we are aware of it or not. We live in a world in which, if we don't classify the situation, the place, or the people around us, we sometimes have trouble expressing ourselves or enjoying our time with other people. We feel uncomfortable if we don't classify everything around us.

I'm not saying that we shouldn't do it at all, but it is important to be aware that we're doing it, and we should understand when we really need to classify others and when we don't.

Life's Scale

Does life exist on a scale?

Is there a natural scale against which we can measure ourselves as good to bad, wise to foolish, and so on?

Do you believe this?

I have noticed that the old version of me—and maybe sometimes the unconscious version of me—felt this way at times.

I am grateful that I'm no longer fixated on the life scale the way I was in the past. Now, I try my best to be conscious as much as I can and to be aware of the moment that my ego asks me to put myself on a scale. I have come to the conclusion that it is my ego that makes me feel that the life scale exists.

You and I and others do not really exist on a scale. Instead, we are units that are related to each other, and together we make one huge, intertwined unit. It's not about measuring yourself or others. It's not about classifying yourself and others. It's about living life and feeling that you are a part of this unit, a part of this world.

My suggestion to you: Whenever you find yourself in a situation in which you feel compelled to say something about yourself or someone else, and you know you are about to classify people on a scale, stop yourself. Ask yourself if it's really necessary, and you are likely to conclude that it is not.

Find the balance zone where you can go inside in this moment and say instead: *We do not exist on a scale. I don't need to say anything that classifies anyone in this way.*

What's important is being in this moment without any resistance and without any need to satisfy your ego — or others around you — by spreading judgment about a situation. Try to catch yourself, and be aware that there is a balanced zone that you can dive into at any time. You can exist in the moment where you don't need to say anything good or bad about you or others.

ARE YOU BETTER OR WORSE THAN OTHERS?

I came to the United States on January 26, 2012.

That first year, I remember how huge the differences were between this country and my country back home, in everything — the culture, the environment, the activities. When you come into a new situation, comparisons and classifications are constant and easy to spot. I remember at that time sitting with different groups of people. In conversations, there were always comparisons between this culture and that — between Arabic culture and Western culture, or Middle Eastern culture and Western culture.

I have noticed that people — everywhere — like to show which is better or worse between two cultures or two countries, and also, between one person and others. Sometimes, within the same group or the same culture, people like to compare who is better and who is worse in a variety of ways; they will talk about who is better at the new language, who adapted to a culture easily, and who had difficulty adapting.

Do You Really Need to Feel That You Are Better or Worse Than Anyone?

I had studied the English language in Pittsburgh, Pennsylvania for four months. When I was in the sixth level of twelve levels of the ESL program, one of my teachers criticized me in front of all the students. I made a grammar mistake in class and she gave me a hard time.

She said, "Razaz, you don't know how to say the sentence correctly. Say, 'She works,' not 'She work.'" Her words directed her disappointment and shame at me for my mistake, which showed me as being the worst student in the class.

At that time, in 2012, I was still learning the language, and it was taking me some time to get the grammar correct. I feel grateful to that teacher now, but when she criticized me that day, I was upset.

I admit, after I left the class, I was crying.

I said to myself: *Oh my gosh, when I was in my country, I could do so many things well! I had a good position then, and now that teacher made me feel like nothing! I can't even get this grammar correct!*

However, I took this situation as a challenge, and I said to myself: *Okay, I'm going to work hard to learn the language, to prove to this teacher that I can do it.*

I set out to be the best in my class.

Later, after I started my master's degree, whenever I remembered that time, I asked myself with a very big smile: *Did I really need to feel that I was better or worse than others or anyone in the class?*

I didn't need to do that—to be competitive with the rest of the class. All that I needed was to feel good about myself, to appreciate my own efforts, whatever I was doing, and to ignore the negative comments from other people.

Whenever you are in a situation in which you are trying hard to accomplish something—develop a skill, improve a relationship—try to look at yourself with this in mind. If you aren't getting what you want or accomplishing what others expect from you, it is easy to focus on how you're measuring up on a scale of some kind. Don't fall into this trap.

Instead, stop and ask yourself: *Do I really need to feel that I am better or worse than anyone?*

You may see that you don't need that, and you may say instead: *What I need to do is be grateful for myself and satisfied about whatever I'm doing because I'm doing the best I can.*

No One Is Better or Worse Than You

When I look at different cultures, I can say confidently that people always have strong opinions about their culture. Some are sure that their culture is the best; no other culture is better. In some situations, they may think that their culture is worse than others, or that other cultures have better value in some way. They may be impressed by what others have accomplished, especially if they could not achieve the same accomplishments. We compare and contrast cultures all the time, the same way we compare people.

That always has made me think about these questions:

- Are some cultures actually better than others?

- Is there really a group that is better than another group?

- Is there really a person who's better than another person?

My answer to these questions is *no*. Each person, each group, has a unique element, a unique set of characteristics. The same applies to every part of life — every situation, circumstance, job, place, home, city.

Something unique has made it what it is. So, we can't say that one is better than another.

There are always differences, but they can't be simply reduced to *better* and *worse*. There are always situations that could work well for you, but couldn't work for others, depending on their ideology, your ideology, their lifestyle, everything they have been through in their past, or everything they are facing right now.

I'm sure that no one is better than you, and you are not better than anyone else. We all have different histories and intentions, and most of us are just doing the best we can.

Say "Thank You" to Your Ego

When you find yourself compelled to compare yourself and others or compare two different people, two different groups, two different countries, or two different cultures, believe me, what pushes you to do that is not you. It's not your truth. It's simply your ego. Your ego is not your soul mind or your soul consciousness. It's your mind's sound; it's your brain's voice.

This voice wants you to match everything on a scale, and say, "Okay, this is better and this is worse. You are good. Others are bad."

Be aware that this tendency always comes from your ego. Any desire to make these comparisons is always motivated by your ego.

All that you need to do is step back a second and say quietly — or even loudly — to yourself: *Thank you, my ego. I don't need to do that.*

Then, just stop and remind yourself: *Every culture, every place, every person is different.*

Remember, always, that the way to control your ego — which means controlling whether you move away or go forward in your comparisons — is to say thank you to your ego.

In doing this, you are saying: *I'm aware of what you are pushing me to do, and I don't need that. I want to enjoy the moment, and I want to enjoy who I am and how others are and enjoy looking at every single group, situation, and person in my life just the way they are.*

Let's go back, once again, to that tightrope walker. Imagine you are carrying something heavy in your hand, and you want to walk forward. You have to keep your balance so you can enjoy walking and can continue passing through the area safely and easily.

You have to be in a balanced state in which you don't let yourself bend to the right or the left side. You have to be focused on how the situation is and on how you are right now, without comparing or classifying yourself or others to the positive side or the negative side. Just remember that you want to be in balance. You want to enjoy the journey with ease and joy.

YOU AND YOURSELF

Sometimes, it may be easier to stop comparing yourself with others if you have reached a certain level of self-confidence and peace, but I truly think that it's harder when it comes to comparing *you* with *yourself*—for example, when you compare your actions today with your actions in a similar situation yesterday.

Are You Allowed to Define Yourself?

After years of different life experiences, working on developing myself, working on always making the best of myself, I am also expanding my consciousness. I've been reading a lot about awareness.

I have found myself in a state in which it's become easy for me to stop comparing myself with others most of the time. But, there have been many times when, subconsciously, I try to define myself to see where I am now or what I am compared to what I have been. On these occasions, I am asking for a definition for myself.

This prompts me to ask other questions:

Are you allowed to define yourself?

Who gives you the permission to define yourself?

Going deeply into my spiritual feeling or relationship with God, I wonder: *If God accepts me as who I am, and God is always with me no matter how I am, and God is always the same with everyone who believes in Him, what is the importance of defining myself?*

We often try to define ourselves. A lot of people on social media, for example, create posts that define themselves. They make their definition a line or two or show a specific image, then share it to spread this definition to let all people look at it so they can demonstrate: *That's who I am.*

Think about it now, just for a second.

Can we really define ourselves this way?

If not, why do we do it?

It's Not about Bad or Good

I remember how I used to teach my daughters — who are now nineteen years old and fifteen years old — that when you look at yourself, it's not about how you are bad or good today. It's about whether you have improved, compared to how you used to be yesterday, or even a month or year ago.

I used to say that a lot. It's about improvement—being a better version of me today, a version that is better than yesterday.

But since early in 2017, I have shifted away from this idea, and I have started teaching my daughters—and myself as well—to keep in mind that it's not about the new version of me that is better than the old version of me from yesterday, or a month or year ago. No!

You don't need to compare yourself with your old self at all.

You don't need to say that you are better or worse than the old version of you, or the version of you from yesterday. You don't even need to be good or better than the version of you from yesterday. So I have quit saying these things completely.

Why shouldn't we focus on comparing ourselves to how we were?

It is because even the old version of you—a year ago, or even three or five years ago— was great. It was the best version of you for that day, in that situation.

When you look at yourself and that version of you yesterday, please don't think about whether it was bad or good or whether you are better or not now. That version of you yesterday was great, and it was the best you in that moment. You don't need to compare yourself to that version. Instead, all that you have to focus on and be aware of is living in this version of you, the new version, having no relationship with the version of you that existed even a minute ago.

The Lover of You

Do you remember a time when you fell in love with something or someone without thinking of what made you feel that way?

You probably felt like this: *Wow, this person or this thing is the greatest, the best! There is no single negative thing I can say about them.*

Whenever people love unconditionally, whenever they are deeply in love, they look only at the positive. They focus only on the best. They don't look at the negative parts at all.

Whenever we admire anything at that level, we experience this high, high energy and a feeling that says, *Oh, this is the best,* no matter what the negatives are.

Imagine if you were that lover yourself—in other words, if you were your own lover, your own greatest fan. If you were, you would never be focusing on negative things about yourself, and you would never hurt yourself by comparing yourself with others.

If you think of yourself this way, you will always have that self-confidence that tells you: *Wow, I am great. I'm beautiful no matter what.*

That can be enough to save you from falling subconsciously into negatively comparing yourself to others, which can instill a lack of self-confidence in you. All that you really have to keep in your mind is being the greatest lover of you — the lover whom you love and who is in love with a completely wonderful person.

You are not better than yourself, and you are not worse than yourself. You don't need to know whether you are better today than who you were yesterday. You don't need to put yourself on a scale of comparison between you and yourself in other situations. All other versions of you are in the past. Be grateful and appreciative of every version of yourself, in *all* your life because each of them was the best it could be in that moment of life.

Self-confidence is what we are all trying to build within ourselves through all our lives, in different ways, while we are learning and working. It's actually simple and very easy to do. You can build your self-confidence yourself if you know how to step back and catch yourself so you can locate the balancing zone between you and others, which is the area in which you can feel yourself stopping from making comparisons.

In this place of balance, you will be able to see clearly that you don't need to make comparisons. No one is better than you, and you are not better than anyone. At the same time, no one is worse than you, and you are not worse than anyone.

No matter what situation you are in, no matter what feelings you are feeling right now — whether it's negative or positive, whether it's satisfying your ego or not — try to remember that, as human beings, we are all a part of one unit, and we're all the same, even if we have outside differences.

We have life circumstances that are different from one another. Everyone is different, but no one is better than the other. Believe me, whenever you find yourself in that balance zone, you will immediately feel that you have confidence in yourself. The truth is that self-confidence is found in simply quitting all the comparing. If you can do that, believe me, you're going to see your self-confidence immediately improving and growing inside of you.

You can imagine being in the zero zone, the balance zone, without any comparing with others and even without any comparing with yourself. This strategy enables you to feed and water the self-confidence seed inside you so it can grow. The more you keep yourself in the balance zone, the more you can water this seed so this plant can flourish and grow.

CHAPTER FOUR

Judgment

RIGHT OR WRONG

Have you ever had a day when you didn't have a need to say: *This is right, or, This is wrong, sometime during the day?*

No matter how hard we try to avoid judgment, we all seem to find ourselves in that situation at times. For some it may not be common—maybe for those who are truly aware of what they are saying and how they are looking at themselves and others. Others may experience twenty-four hours of nonstop judgment.

Nothing Is Right

I remember when I was a graduate student at Florida Institute of Technology in Melbourne, Florida, and studying for my masters in global strategy communication, I had a class in which we were discussing global marketing.

My professor often used to say, "There is nothing right or wrong; there are only differences."

I remember the first time she said that. It was kind of a shock to me because even though I had heard this kind of idea before and I had read it many times, her statement came at a moment in my life that made it very significant to me.

I remember saying it over to myself: *Okay, there is nothing right . . . ?*

I stopped at that specific part and I wondered: *If there are a lot of things that the majority of us can look at and agree are right — or wrong — how is my professor now saying there is nothing right or wrong?*

However, when I started paying more and more attention to this idea and looked at it from my life point — examining myself, and also looking at others around me — I figured out that it's true that nothing is right. This doesn't mean that since it's not right, it's wrong. No. I can say nothing is right *or* wrong.

I know that when I don't label a decision I have made — or something I have done — as right, it makes it possible that tomorrow I can change my mind. Tomorrow I may find something better, or decide to go a different way.

Does that mean that what I did first was wrong?

No, but at the same time, I wouldn't call it right, either.

What you may think of as right might not be. What nearly all people around us agree is right might, for some people, be wrong. Something can be right in the current moment, but for another day in the future, it could be wrong. I don't believe that anything is ever 100 percent right.

Just be aware. If you feel that something is right, it's okay—no problem—but don't be very tied to the idea of it being right.

What Does "Wrong" Mean?

"There is nothing right or wrong; there are only differences."

Going back to the moment I heard that in my classroom when I was a graduate student, I remember wondering: *What does wrong mean?*

You can ask yourself this question now. Give yourself a minute just to think about it.

What does wrong mean to you?

When we say that something is wrong in a situation, I don't think it's about the situation itself, or the person involved, or whatever happened. It's not even about the ideas involved. It's about our feeling toward wherever we are releasing the judgment.

For example, if you see two people on the beach or in the mall, and they are demonstrating some kind of bad behavior — based on what you think is bad — you might say something like:

- *Oh, that's really wrong.*
- *That's a wrong attitude.*
- *Oh, they shouldn't talk to each other like that.*

You are feeling something is wrong with what you are seeing, but what do you mean by *wrong?*

Actually, there is nothing wrong in the situation, but there is a feeling that came out of *you.* You did not like what you saw.

You can apply this to your own behavior.

If you do something and then you say to yourself: *Oh, I did something wrong. I think I shouldn't talk to my sister this way,* you are not talking about what actually happened.

You are talking about your own feelings about what happened.

Your feelings are something completely different from the situation itself. When you realize this, it makes a huge difference in your perception — in your attitude toward whatever happens to you, or in front of you — because you have that wall between you and what's going on.

What you may see as wrong, in another time, or another period of your life, you may find yourself accepting today. If you go back to, let's say, a period in your life ten years or so ago, you may find that you used to disagree with something, but now you have totally the opposite point of view. You may now like this idea; you may have adopted a different position now. It wasn't wrong, the way you labeled it at that moment. It just was something that you didn't accept. It simply didn't fit your feelings.

Differences Are a Fact

Looking at *right* or *wrong* as the result of any judgment naturally leads us to try to find facts to support our judgment.

However, when you judge something as right, this judgment isn't automatically considered a fact, and the same is true when you say something is wrong. The only real fact you can find in this situation is the fact that differences exist between people.

It is possible for you and I to both judge the same thing at the same moment. Let's say you feel that it's right and I feel that it's wrong, and both of us say what we think.

However, where are the facts in this situation?

If I say, "Oh, now the weather is very hot, and it's not a good time to go out in the sun."

You might say, "No, it's a perfect time to enjoy being under the sun."

What is fact?

Is it what I said?

Is it what you said?

Actually, I don't think either one of them is fact.

The fact is the difference that comes from all of us. Whenever you find yourself judging something and labeling it right or wrong, remind yourself that this is not a fact. It's just one potential of unlimited potentials in this universe or in this life. Remember that the fact is, there are differences, but there is nothing right or wrong.

I know it's not easy to avoid moments when you may, consciously or subconsciously, say, *This is right,* or, *This is wrong,* whether it's something about you or others or a situation you have in your life. When it happens, stop and pull yourself back to the balance point or the zero point in the judgment.

Stay there for a second, inside you, and say to yourself: *You know, it's not right or wrong. It's just how it is.*

Try to hold yourself there. Just stay in that balance and observe from a place where you can see the whole picture instead of being immersed in the situation.

WHO'S THE JUDGE?

Many times in my life, I have wanted to appoint myself as a judge for a situation in my life. I think this is true for many other people as well. I wanted to be able to decide whether it was right or wrong, good or bad. I wanted to decide whether it should be as it is or it should be changed.

When people ask for my opinion, I find I sometimes want to make a judgment.

I have come to realize that the judge shouldn't be me.

If the judge shouldn't be me, then I have to ask myself: *Who should the judge be?*

Who is the judge?

Are You God?

At times, I have thought that the judge should be someone wiser than me, someone, for example, older than me or more educated. Maybe it should be someone outside of the situation.

I have wondered: *Okay, if it's not me and if it's not someone wiser than me, then who should be the judge?*

The only one who can truly be a judge is God. God didn't ask us to judge ourselves. God created us to be on a journey of development, not on a journey of judgment. God did not create us to sit in judgment of ourselves or others. Focusing on this idea has helped me to sit back whenever I find myself wanting to judge a situation or a person.

I ask myself: *Am I God, to do that?*

Asking this question makes me realize that I am not meant to judge because I'm a human being. Whatever the situation, I am immersed in the human process of changing, getting better—simply doing the best I can.

When you have questions about making judgments, just ask yourself: *Are you God?*

Listen to the answers that will come to you. You may discover and find more answers than what I have given. There is a lot to figure out and be aware of, more than what I can say.

What Does "Wrong" Mean?

I would like you to think about something that happened with you today, yesterday, or even a week ago. Try to remember a moment when you judged someone—

especially in a relationship — and that judgment turned the whole situation negative so that you lost your joy in that moment.

Most of us have done this with regularity, whether it is once a month, once a week, or even once a day. How often depends on how aware you are, how easily you judge, and how well you are able to avoid being in this kind of situation.

I strongly believe wherever this kind of judgment arises, joy can't exist at all. This is especially true when it's a negative judgment in our relationships, particularly in our very close relationships like family or friends.

In any situation in which there is a disagreement, or when you feel anger or frustration, you always have a choice — and often, there are many choices.

Here are some options to consider:

- You can free yourself by accepting this moment and deciding not to say or do anything.

- You can act like a child, releasing all judgments, moving forward in fun and joy like nothing happened.

- You can just simply release any judgment — even judgments that seem small or minor — and thank yourself for making the good choice.

Let us say, for example, you have a problem with something your husband, wife, boyfriend, or girlfriend did, and then you say to them, "Oh, I wish you wouldn't do that. I think that is not right."

Believe it or not, the ego is always ready to take that defensive stance. Whenever the ego starts showing up, then the moment between two people starts losing that positive, happy vibration of love and peace. Both people are going to start thinking about who is right or wrong. There can be no joy in the situation, even if it doesn't go to a very negative extreme. There is no way to keep the situation on the positive side; it will only be able to vibrate back and forth on the negative side.

Judgment Is Fake

Judgment is fake. Just look with me at any situation where you make a judgment of right or wrong, or good or bad, and then ask two or three people. Notice how everyone has a difference of ideas—a different judgment—about the same things at the same moment. Trying to find a majority agreement on one side or your self-proof for a situation on the other side is just wasting time. You are trying to convince yourself that something needs to be classified or have an identification, but, in the reality of your higher awareness, there is nothing that needs to be identified and nothing that needs to be judged as right or wrong.

I say that judgment is fake for many reasons.

When you make a judgment:

- You can so easily change your mind by changing your perception.

- You can be relying on facts that turn out to be false.

- You can change your mind.

- You can figure out that you misunderstood something when you made your judgment.

- Additional information can come to light afterward, and you may think: *Oh, my goodness! How did I not think about this? This is not right; this is wrong!*

There is a high potential that whenever you judge something, your judgment might be fake, or worse—your judgment could keep you from seeing what could be better for you and for others.

DO WE NEED A JUDGE?

Most of us—if not all—find ourselves in this judgment situation every day or at least once a week. For example, sometimes my husband and I have a moment like a lot of couples when each one of us wants to show that he or she is right and the other person is wrong. Subconsciously, when a couple is in a strong argumentative state, both people usually think they should agree or disagree. Each person thinks the situation needs a final judgment.

I remember how I started to change my attitude. I started asking questions inside of myself whenever I argued with my husband.

I asked myself:

- *Who is the judge in this situation?*
- *Do we really need a judge?*
- *Does the situation really need a final judgment?*
- *Do we truly need to say one of us is right and the other one is wrong?*

Time after time, I have realized the minute I ask myself these questions that the answer to each of them is *no*. I immediately feel happy because I can relax and accept whatever he's saying, which allows any argument to end peacefully.

Who's the Life Judge?

Recently, in the last part of this chapter, I mentioned that God is the only judge. That's what I believe; however, you may think that we often need a judge in life to help us with whatever situations are happening between people—in court or at work, for example. At the same time, as I've said, I'm still figuring out whether we need a judge, especially in our relationships.

Part of me is convinced that we don't need one. However, in life, there are two parts: There is the life we are actively living in, day by day, and there are the situations and the people around us.

I want you to examine these questions and to think past what I am saying right now. I want you to look at perspectives that are different from mine, to look further than what I can see, to go deeper and seek *your* truth.

What Does Your Ego Need?

When you judge, usually it's not the deepest part of you doing the judging. It's not your spirit. It's not your soul. The one who judges is your ego. The soul or the spirit is created to be in harmony with everything in this life — to be *the life* in this life — because it's absolutely connected with God.

When your ego is active, when it has control, you start using your mind more. This makes you want to analyze everything, classify everything, and judge everything, even if the situation doesn't require it.

I remember when my husband and I were riding our bikes, and I had my little son with me in a bike trailer. He was four months old. We stopped by our neighbor's house to say hi. I remember that I picked up my son from his trailer, and I started going toward my neighbor to give her my son. As I started to hand her the baby, she was freaking out.

She said, "Oh, no, I can't hold him! I have never held any baby in my life!"

She had been married for more than thirty years, but she hadn't had any kids, and she was really freaking out. She didn't want to hold my son; she didn't even want to say hi to him!

Now, I have some background knowledge of psychology, and my mind quickly turned to analyzing mode. Maybe there was a psychological reason for her behavior. Maybe she had a problem related to a situation with babies. It was a fast conversation; it happened in less than fifteen seconds. These thoughts came immediately; they wanted to say something inside of me; they wanted to find an excuse for what I was seeing.

I didn't speak my thoughts aloud. All this happened silently inside of me.

The thoughts weren't negative—I had very positive intentions—I was trying to understand, to find a reason why she didn't want to hold my son, why she freaked out and drew away from me.

Still, why should I judge, say, or interpret what happened?

Why?

In a matter of seconds, I stopped myself.

Inside me, I said: *Razaz, stop! You don't need to say why she's doing that. Just enjoy the moment! Just enjoy the feeling that you, your husband, and your son, all of you are with your neighbor, laughing and enjoying this moment.*

It was a very conscious act. I stopped myself and forced my attention to focus on the moment instead of focusing on judging.

I continue to try to do this same thing whenever I feel that I'm trying to say something that is a judgment, even if it's only inside of me, even if it's a positive and not a negative. I stop myself because I'm aware that it's not my soul or my spirit who is talking in this kind of situation. It's not my soul or my spirit who is enjoying this moment. It's actually my ego.

The ego always wants to find a reason.

It wants to find anything that makes me feel: *Okay, you are truly understanding the situation. You are truly understanding this person. Now, you can be truly happy about this situation.*

Your ego has these kinds of needs. Be aware that any judgment—any judge—always has an ego behind it that wants to take an action to satisfy a need. There is a reason that your ego acts.

Always ask yourself, in any judgment situation, whether it's between you and yourself, or you and others:

Why are you moved to judgment?

What is it that your ego needs at this moment?

Judge That You Don't Judge

> *The mind is everything. What you think, you become.*
> ~ Buddha

Talking about judgment or looking at judgment from a theoretical perspective is very easy. You might agree that we shouldn't judge, or we don't need to judge, and that it's important to be aware when we are judging ourselves, or others—but actually applying these changes in our lives may not be as easy.

Let your actions adapt to this idea. Start by becoming aware. Be aware of the moments when you are judging anything and ask yourself if you need to judge. If you answer that judgment isn't necessary, the next step is stopping yourself. I know it's not easy, but it's possible.

Keep these words in mind: *Be aware and stop judging.*

I have found this very simple statement to be helpful and supportive. Whenever you feel that there is no way to avoid judging a person or a situation, or you feel that you can't really control your ego, make this statement as a reminder. Write it as a note in your journal or notebook.

Remind yourself whenever you feel that you want or need to judge:

> *Judge not, lest you be judged.*
> Matthew 7:1, ESV

We all have different ideas, and we have different answers for whether we need a judge or not and for whom we should be a judge in any situation. But, I'm sure that no matter what your answer is, there is always a way to hold yourself back, to keep yourself in that peace moment, in that balance where you can choose not to act in a judgmental way.

At least make an effort to become aware that you really don't need to judge anything until you figure out whether you need a judge or not.

My main purpose in talking about judgment is just to let you be aware or to remind you that judgment—

most of the time, if not all the time — is your ego voice. It's not your spirit. It's not your soul.

There is nothing right or wrong; anything could be right or wrong or neither one of them. The fact is that there are always differences, even between you and yourself, even between you and the moment that you are in right now.

In order to enjoy your life, try as much as you can to avoid judgment, to quit listening to your ego. Try not to allow your ego to say something about everything. Just try it for at least an hour in the day, and see how you feel. Remember, whatever your judgment, it's not what the issue is that matters most; it's the *feeling* about it that is most important.

Judging Your Relationships

Remember, your relationships with others are the compilation of countless moments. If you find yourself in one moment — or more — that you don't like, please don't judge all your moments with that person on that basis.

Instead of judging someone or your relationship, look deeply at the loving moments, and be grateful for them, because that is what is going to allow you either to continue with that person, or to let them go out of your life peacefully.

Judging can easily make you unable to continue happily with someone, but it can also make you stick with someone you are not meant to be with; it can make it impossible to let them go.

Judgments on the Tightrope

I have mentioned in each chapter the example of the tightrope walker. Once again, envision yourself on the tightrope. I want you to see yourself when you judge something.

Where are you and where *could* you be?

How can you move, walk, and continue your journey?

The more you let your ego judge, the more you will be leaning to one side on that tightrope, even if you stay positive.

And how about negativity?

Negativity is going to impact you even more.

Imagine yourself on that tightrope, doing whatever you can do to be in that balance, avoiding judgment, and focusing on the importance of the moment. Imagine what it would be like to walk the tightrope. Imagine what your life would be like if you were balanced and confident in the moment.

How would it feel?

Find balance and you can enjoy your life, enjoy your relationships, and enjoy observing yourself developing from one situation to the next. You will be able to observe, without judgment, the beauty of all the changes around you from moment to moment.

CHAPTER FIVE

Money

DO YOU REALLY NEED MONEY, OR DOES MONEY NEED YOU?

I grew up in a family where all my needs were taken care of, and I didn't need to think about money. I grew up just thinking about what I could do with my life as a student, and later, as a wife and a mother.

The Arabic culture makes a woman think about her family and her responsibility as a woman more than as someone who makes money. Even though she might work or might have a business, the most important thing for her is not to think about the money, but to think about her family and what she can do for them. I have not had to worry about money during my life, even here in the United States. As a graduate student, I was supported by scholarships and my dad.

Everything was paid. I was just enjoying the money without considering whether I was going to need more. I was used to feeling supported; I never had to think about money.

However, when I graduated in 2015, I thought: *Okay, now I'm living here in the United States, not in Saudi Arabia – where I used to work, but I wasn't focused on work or money. I want to start my own financial life, where I know that I am supported, but at the same time, I want to feel that I am making the money.*

At the same time, I wanted to start teaching my daughters about money as they grew up. It was such an important moment of awareness when I realized I hadn't learned what money really was. I hadn't learned how to make it or how to support myself, financially.

So how could I teach these things to my daughters?

Value Yourself

How should I talk to my children about the value of money?

All their lives, I had been teaching my daughters that nothing has more value than you and yourself. As they grew up, however, they started thinking about money more, even though they had enough money, and they were living in an Arabic society where they didn't need to think about money.

Because of social media, which expanded what they could see of the world, they were impacted by many new ideas. They saw many examples of women who were successful in different careers — from models to scientists to businesswomen.

When my daughters were teenagers — the oldest about seventeen years old, and the second one about thirteen years old — they started to have questions:

- *How do we make money?*
- *Could we become business women?*
- *How could we get that huge amount of money in our bank accounts?*

The questions in my mind were in different terms.

- *Do they really need the money?*
- *Does the money need them to make a difference in a life?*

I have a saying that I often use: *Before you think about money, think about yourself.*

I've always advised others, including my children, to begin this way because when you value yourself, you have a good place to start making sense of everything else. If you can't value yourself, you couldn't value anything else, including money. Money can't make anything without you.

Do You Want Money, or Do You Want to Be Rich?

One day, I was talking with my older daughter, who was eighteen at the time. I asked her about her dreams.

"What do you want to be?"

She said she wanted to be a designer or a makeup artist and had many other ideas as well. She said that one of the reasons that she wanted to have one of these careers was that she wanted to be rich. She wanted to have a lot of money.

Then a question came to my mind immediately, and I asked her, "Which is it you really want? Do you want money? Or do you want to be rich?"

Being rich and *having money* are completely different ideas. No matter how much money you have, you can be rich. At the same time, you may have millions or billions in your bank account and not be rich at all. Richness is not about money. Money is a number and it's important. We all love numbers, but it doesn't determine richness in life.

I'd love to have as much money as I can, even more than what I can ever imagine. But, richness is a different situation. Richness, in my point of view, is a communication of value, of emotions. Richness is not what you have; it's what you feel. It is both what you feel generally and what you feel specifically about what you have in your life.

Imagine you have little money, and you have a neediness in your approach to your life. In this case, you are lacking money and lacking richness as well.

Now, imagine that you have a million dollars in the bank, or a billion, but you still have that needy emotion inside of you. In this case, you're just focused on looking for more. You're not satisfied with what you have.

You are constantly thinking: *What more can I have?*

You have a great deal of money, but are you rich?

I don't think that could ever be a rich situation. You are rich when you feel that you are happy with what you have. You can give, and you can enjoy what you have no matter how much it is.

Whenever you think about money, ask yourself these questions to get clarity about the issue of money in your life:

Do I really need money?

Is it about having more money, or is it about being rich?

Can Money Work for You?

When most people work for a company, they feel that they are working for the money. If you ask them why they are working, most people would answer that they want to make money, accumulate savings, or pay for particular purchases.

For most people, their motivation is all related to money. Indirectly, you could say that they feel as if the *money* is their boss. They try to keep their job and do their best because they are worried about what is going to happen with the money. They are not worried about what is going to happen with the company itself, but with the money — although this doesn't mean that the same person couldn't have loyalty to the company they are working for.

What I'm saying is that, for most people, the priority is money so it doesn't matter what happens in the company. If they feel that their money is coming in well, they feel okay. It feels like they are working *for* the money. If money is tight, they may feel like a slave to their paycheck.

Imagine if, while you are working for a company and receiving a salary, you think of money working for *you* instead. What if you go to work each day so that money will work toward your list of wants and desires? What if your job is your way to *hire* money, to be the boss?

Would this change the way you looked at your employment?

Would you do anything differently?

If you know the answer, you may have a better understanding of the money and of yourself. It doesn't matter whether you are an employee or not. What matters is whether you can be the boss of the money for your own benefit, wherever you are working. Subconsciously, that's what I was doing when I was working for a company in Saudi Arabia for many years, mainly because I wasn't thinking a lot about making money.

Imagine if you can subconsciously feel: *I'm here at work so money will work for me. The money is asking me to be there. The work is asking me to be there, because I can be anywhere; it doesn't matter.*

Take a moment to think about it.

I want to say honestly to you that I'm still learning how to make money. I'm still learning how to deal with money using a different perspective than what I used to have, and I'm enjoying this new challenge. I understand that, as long as we are alive, we will be trying new things, making improvements, and learning different skills.

From my point of view right now, one of the most important questions that I'm answering for my learning process is: *Do I work for money or does money work for me?*

A related question is: *Do I really need money, or does money need me?*

To be honest, sometimes, no matter what fulfillment we may have, it's human nature to have a desire for more, and we may always ask for more. There are times when we need money, or we think that we need money.

Whenever it comes to this point, and you feel that you really need money, ask yourself that question: *Do I really need money, or does money need me?*

Ask the question because, when you think about it, you may find that the answer is the opposite of what you think.

ARE YOU POOR OR RICH?

I remember the first time I read the 1997 book, *Rich Dad, Poor Dad,* by Robert Kiyosaki. That book is one of the books that changed my thinking about money in a major way.

It has helped me examine the way that I deal with money, and at the same time, it has made me think a lot about these questions:

How do we determine if someone is poor or rich?

Can we say if someone else is poor or rich?

I have even asked myself, based on a lot of what I read in this book: *Am I poor or rich?*

Define Your Bank Statement

What does your bank statement mean to you?

Some people feel that it tells how much they have or don't have. Maybe some think that it classifies their financial situation; for example, it tells whether they are rich or they are poor. Maybe some have another perspective or attach a different meaning to the bank statement. I have asked myself, many times, about a definition for my bank statement.

I've done some research. After reading many books about various issues — like how to deal with money, what money means, and how to get your money to work for you — I feel that, although the numbers are very important, it's more complicated than that.

Your bank statement is not only about the numbers, but also about the improvements you can make with money and the creativity you can apply to increase your money.

I started looking at my bank statement to see the numbers printed there, but more importantly, I look at the bank statement as an *improvement statement.* I try to observe and notice the improvements between one month and another. It's not about what I have, because honestly, sometimes I may have lots of money — for example, I may have received money from my dad as a gift — but it can easily be spent in one day. I've come to think that it's about improvement, whatever that means to you.

I define my bank statement in this way, by the improvements over time. Defining the bank statement can help you make a plan by giving you a kind of scale to understand more of what's going on and by helping you define your attitude about the money.

Classify Your Value

I always try to avoid judging, classifying, or applying definitions for most things in my life. But when it comes to money, how to use it in your life, how to value money, or how to deal with it, this is always an uncomfortable situation that requires some thought.

Ask appropriate and thoughtful questions, like:

- *What is the value of my money?*

- *Does money have more value than taking care of the family or finishing up some obligation?*

It comes down to how you value money and other things in your life. Most of the time, you are making these choices, consciously or subconsciously, whether you know it or not — but you want your values to direct these actions. Instead of being unconscious of your intentions in your life, instead of acting subconsciously about money and making it have more value than whatever else you have in your life, take some time and think about classifying your values.

To classify your values, you first have to know what your values are. Without including money, list them in order from one to ten, and see where they fall in terms of your priorities. After you do this, it's time to involve the money. Insert money into your list as something that can help you to increase one of your other values or to use to support your values.

In this way, you won't be listing money as a value that can be compared with any other value — for example, love, family, or spirituality — but it can be applied to enhance your life by supporting what you value.

Never Poor or Rich

A few days ago, just before I started writing this passage, I watched an interview in which Oprah Winfrey interviewed Lynne Twist, author of the 2010 book, *The Soul of Money: Transforming Your Relationship with Money and Life.* In just the few minutes I watched the show, it had an impact on me.

I don't know for sure if it was a message given to me to add to this book or not, but I consider it a message. I already had written the outline for this book, and the writer was talking about a point that I felt was very important.

What I understood from her in a couple of minutes of this interview is that really no one is poor or rich. That really struck a chord with me.

I thought: *Oh, my goodness! Finally, there is someone who is talking about what I believe in!*

I always believed that it's not about someone being poor or someone being rich. What she was saying — and it's amazing how it is exactly what I believe in — is that there is simply a situation with money. For example, there is no poor person, but there is a person who has a poor situation with money, or there is a person who happens to have a lack of money.

From my point of view — and this is what I already have talked about in the previous chapter — you can't judge anyone, because what might be right to you might not be right from someone else's perspective. For example, there were times in my life when I knew some poor people — meaning I may have called them poor or society may have called them poor. However, when I sat and talked with them, it didn't seem at all like they were poor. Some of these people had a high, rich feeling; they were not focused on wanting more money. They felt that they were satisfied by what they had, and they really loved the life they lived.

If you told them, "I want to give you one million dollars," I would not be surprised to hear them say, "No, I'm happy."

They may tell you, simply, "No, I'm happy with what I have."

You may say that they are poor, but at the same time, they don't really feel that they are poor because they don't have any need for more money. They feel that what they have is the best.

I'm not saying that they are right or wrong, but they may have a belief, from the background that formed them, that rich people are bad people or unhappy people. This makes them happy with what they have, and they don't want more.

So, is it your right to classify people and say that they are poor?

Is it your right to classify people and say that they are rich?

I don't think so, from my point of view, but you may find others who disagree.

I hope to read Twist's book soon to have a better understanding, or hopefully, to discover more about what a financial situation tells about a relationship between the person and the money.

I suggest you ask yourself the same question that I'm asking myself.

Whenever you have any financial situation, or any thought about money, just ask yourself in that moment, in the feeling you feel, "Are you poor or rich?"

But remind yourself that you are not asking this question based on your relationship with the money. No, it's about your relationship with yourself.

Do you have a poor feeling, a needy feeling?

Or do you have a sense of fulfillment inside of you — do you feel rich?

YOUR FINANCIAL SPIRITUALITY

As I told you previously, in recent years, I have been learning about how to deal with money, asking questions like:

What does money mean?

How can I make my own wealth, not depending on my dad's wealth?

In this journey of learning, I have been observing and considering finances and spirituality, or financial situations and spirituality. My journey has taken me into many different areas.

One day, I was watching some photos and videos on social media that inspired me to be more aware of the relationship between the different parts of the energy centers within the human body, which are called chakras. As it's known, each chakra has its own vibrational frequency and a lot of people think about the root chakra's activation as a powerful way to enhance their relationship with money.

But if you think about how the cooperation between anything and everything in the world could enhance or change the quality of our materialistic world, you will realize that there is something missing in what many people do when they focus on the root chakra in any financial situation.

I think in order to manifest more money in your life, it's not enough to depend on clearing and activating the root chakra because you can receive more money easily and frequently by activating your crown chakra as well. This cooperation between the crown chakra and root chakra can give you a higher result in any financial situation because you combine the power of your higher self with the power of the flow of the Universe.

Mentally, I considered how our bodies are created with greatness and creativity—how our non-physical and physical existence and parts are connected. The chakra that is related to spirituality—the crown chakra—is in harmony with the one that is related to physical desires—the root chakra—if we are in balance.

I considered this great relationship between these two chakras and the importance of being in balance to activate them both. That day, I observed many things about money in my personal life and in others as I searched for a deeper understanding.

The Connection

Have you discovered the relationship between your spirit, your soul, and your money?

There is a connection between them. I have observed so many different types of people in life; for example, you may find some who are rich but unhappy, some who are rich and happy, and some who are not rich and not happy. There are all of these different kinds of people, and I have tried to draw some meaning from my observations.

I've asked myself many questions about how different people feel about their lives, and what makes them happy.

What is the one thing that makes you feel comfortable?

What makes you feel like you really have balance in your life?

I have noticed that the happiest people are those who have a good connection between their money and their spirit. In other words, they have a great *financial spirituality*, which means they place a high value on being a spiritual person. These people generally are full of love and enjoy giving. They are people who place high value on peace, and they believe in God, although this belief may manifest in very different ways. They can be Christian. They can be Muslim. They can be in any religion.

It's not about the religion. It's about having the spiritual connection between the person and God and having, at the same time, a good connection between living life and having needs, desires, and dreams that need money. These people feel a rich feeling, a fulfilled feeling, because they have that good connection between spirituality and money. This is financial spirituality.

A person with great financial spirituality understands that in order to have a higher and better financial situation, you have to keep improving the other side, your spiritual situation, or the spiritual part of you. As long as you're keeping and improving both of these together, you will be happy. No matter how much money you have, no matter how rich you are, the most important ingredient is how you feel toward what you have.

Does God Exist in the Money?

As a person who believes in God, I believe that God exists in everything. It is God who has created everything in this life, in this universe — including me. So when we consider money, here is the question to ask:

Does God exist in the money?

I don't know how I came up with this question, but I have asked it of myself many times. I'd love for you to ask yourself and find your own answer. It's not about religion, as I said before. It's about your spirituality. No matter what your beliefs are about God, just think about it.

God's Grace Through Your Money

If the money is one of the things through which we can feel God, or we can see God's power or God's light in our life, it means that money is not that difficult. Money is not the light, but the light is God. The power is in God because the money comes to us through God. For example, you may sit in your home, and then you might get a call.

Someone on the phone might ask you, "Could you please do this job with me?" and then offer you a promotion, or a commission, just like that.

Think about it: How did that person call you and give you that offer?

Do you think that it's just the person by themselves?

Do you think that it's a coincidence?

I don't think so.

I believe that there is no such thing as coincidence. Everything is happening according to a very precise plan.

Your financial spirituality means, in my point of view, that there is a connection between God and money, or there is a connection between prosperity or abundance and God. It's not just about how you can get the money or what you can do with the money. It's something higher than that. It's true power. It can be used to make a difference in your life, for you as a body, and for your spirit.

As I said before, the more you have spirituality, or you have that sense of spirituality and a great relationship with God, the more you can have a financially happy life. You can observe or notice some different types of people you have known and see that this is true.

There are people in the middle class who feel that they are rich because they know how to use the money, and they are using the money to serve the people around them. They are serving society as well as serving their family. In doing this, they ascend to a higher spirituality level, and that gives them more happiness. They believe that the more they give money, the more their money is going to come back to them.

At the same time, there are very rich people who have the same perspective. They are super rich, and they are very happy. They never think about whether they may lose some money. They accept that even if they lose money, they can get it back, and they can always—no matter how rich they are—forget about everything, thinking about themselves in the moment and enjoying the money.

They are always thinking more and more about how they can serve others and how they can make this life better and different. Bill Gates is an example, and you can find many others. You can see how they have great projects developed solely to serve others.

Whenever you think about money, or whenever you deal with money, you have to be conscious and aware of many things. Money can be a tool for your life, and it can help you serve others, as we have discussed, but it can also become something that controls you. It can pull you to feel that you are rich, or it can pull you to feel that you are poor. What I want you to do is to find and maintain your balance — like the tightrope walker we've used as an example in every chapter.

Imagine that you are the tightrope walker, and you are thinking that you are poor or rich.

Do you think that you can maintain balance well enough to walk, to continue the journey?

I don't think so. You will be leaning to one side, unbalanced. If you think the opposite, it's the same. Here is where people lose the happiness in their life. They lose the joy because they are thinking about whether they are poor or rich, whether they have a lot of money or less money, and they let the money control them.

My point here is that you must control the money; don't let it control you. Whenever you have any financial situation in which you are dealing with money, remember that you are controlling the money. If you are the tightrope walker, this doesn't mean that your job is just to think about the money. No. Instead, think about how to find and keep the balance.

If you want to find your balance zone, your zero zone, or your joy zone—the comfortable zone you can be in—remember your financial spirituality. The more you have a great connection with God, the more you fulfill your energy, and the more you take care of the point energy in your body—which is related to your spirituality—the more you can have a good relationship with not only the money but with all of the abundance in your life.

Just take care of both sides, not thinking you have to be either this or that. Find the balance where you are not thinking about being a giving person and a spiritual person, but you are living your actual life, with an awareness of the moment. If you have that great connection with God, and you have a great financial spirituality, then peace and happiness will follow, because the balance exists in you.

Money is a situation that depends on your relationship with God!

No matter what your definition of God is, your relationship with God shapes your self-image and worth and programs your subconscious mind. Whether you consider God the lord of your religion, the source of everything, the creator of the universe, the core of your beliefs, a guide or supporter, pure energy through you, or something else, this relationship fills your heart with trust and confidence. This is what you need to manifest the money you want and to enjoy it.

Money is one of the spontaneous results of your relationship with God. Pay attention that your rituals actually connect you with God. Being able to recite prayers, for example, doesn't necessarily mean that you have a great relationship with God.

If you express an intention, consider it the intention of God. How then could you doubt that it could be fulfilled?
~ Vadim Zeland

Conclusion

One morning, something powerful happened to me. I remember waking up very early in the morning to a voice inside of me repeating: *There is no time – there is no time – there's no time – there is only now.*

I don't remember what I was dreaming that night. I don't know if that voice was a continuation of the dream, or if it was my higher consciousness that wanted to help me to believe in the power of the moment. As I made my way through my morning routine – taking a shower, feeding my baby, taking a walk – I remember that I kept repeating those same sentences every couple minutes.

There is no time – there is no time – there's no time – there is only now.

Even though, for many years, I had been reading about the power of living in the moment, and I had expanded my consciousness to focus on living in the moment, when I woke up repeating those sentences that day, I felt something different I can't even explain.

That experience affected me deeply. From it, I now understand that I only have this moment. I understand that it is in this moment that I can make everything and enjoy everything and be connected to God and to all the potentials of the universe.

A few weeks later, I started the process of writing this book.

I have a lot to say, but nothing is more important than saying this: *Love this moment – love to experience it – love to live it.*

Life is not a moment, but in a moment, you can find life. In order to enjoy the moment, and the life you want, remember to keep yourself in balance. Whenever you are in balance, it means that you are satisfied about whatever you are doing and with whatever you have. Life is not about accomplishing the most or being in the most fascinating places. Life is about really feeling the moment.

Remind yourself whenever you are distracted by anything—whether it is the pain of the past or the worry of the future—remind yourself that you are here, and now is the time to live life. Live your life by your own truth. Don't think about what this truth is, or how great it is, but live in it. Enjoy it because the more you enjoy it, the more you can develop it. Strive to feel the emotions that create your good vibrations in order to stay continually where you are—or move toward better.

Being in balance doesn't require lots of action. It's just steps of awareness. It is a moment of consciousness that you can return to whenever you feel the need. For example, if you are ready to fall into your past or your future, you can take action for a second and restore yourself to the moment. If you are in a judgment situation, remind yourself that you are not better or worse than anyone, and no one is better or worse than you. Then you can find peace between you and others, you and yourself, or you and any situation you are in.

All that you need is a second of action to remind yourself. If you are out of balance, this reminder can stop you for a moment so you can return to find the feeling of safety, the gratitude, the quiet, and the calm mind. This is how you can let your own soul or spirit help you enjoy your life's mission.

Keep in mind the importance of being aware and conscious. Strive to always be aware, but be particularly conscious at significant moments when you may need to take a position or where you may find yourself out of balance.

Take action at these times by first asking yourself: *Where is my balance zone?*

The zero zone — the balance zone — is the area where everything has no measurement. Everything has no judgment. *Where* you are is connected to *who* you are. It is connected with your highest consciousness and with your truth. In this zone, you will always find a way to enjoy your life and to enjoy it in each moment.

Don't think of your life *as a moment;* instead, live your life *in the moment.* If you can do this, you are always going to find something beautiful and real to enjoy, and to live with, whether it's inside you or it's around you. You can find all this in the balance zone because when you find balance, you will have the ability to be in the moment, where there is nothing more or less than the beautiful second in which you are living.

So, imagine I am asking you at this moment, "Where are you now?" Imagine taking a selfie of this moment.

What is your answer?

Whether you answered with an actual space and time or your location in the non-physical world, this question pulled you back into your balance zone, the place where I wish you continued joy on your journey.

Next Steps

I believe that everyone and everything can teach and inspire me and this makes me ever thankful for everything and everyone I have in my life. If you have enjoyed this book, please share your comments with me through social media. I'm so happy and grateful to receive your feedback. Thank you.

To find out more, feel free to contact me in one of the following ways:

Email: Razaz.now@gmail.com.

Twitter: Razaz_Banoun

Instagram: @razaz.banoun

Phone: 321-368-2419

About the Author

Razaz Banoun was born in Lahour, Pakistan, but raised in Saudia Arabia. She received her bachelor's degree in sociology from King Adjulaziz University in Jeddah, Saudi Arabia, graduating with honors. In 2012, she moved to the United States to learn the English language and to attend Florida Institute of Technology (FIT) where she received a master's degree in global strategic communication in December, 2015.

She is an inspirational woman who has achieved much in her life, including three great kids, but she is most proud of the 2008 award she received from A-Shafi School, which her daughters attended in Saudi Arabia, for being an Idealistic Mom. She believes that an idealistic mother is the mother who never tries to be perfect, but instead, loves to grow with her kids and enjoy the moment spontaneously and consciously.

Razaz loves to encourage people to use their work and attitude as their main language. She uses her experience with the English language as an example for other people. Even though she only started learning English in 2012, she received an award for Outstanding Academic Performance at FIT for the academic year, 2013–2014.

Razaz Banoun is the founder of Razaz Life Counseling, personal counselor, and an inspirational speaker. She teaches many online courses and has been represented in many workshops: *The Consciousness of Spiritual Communication, The Consciousness of Love and Romance, The Consciousness of Confidence, Choice Journey, Awareness of Ego & the Secrets of Dealing with It, Pregnancy and Childbirth, Consciously & Enjoy,* and *Nurture Is Consciousness and Light.*

She has also written for a national newspaper in the United Arab Emirates. She is currently a mentor who focuses on raising and increasing the level of consciousness for whomever needs it.

Razaz is in love with God, kids, meditation, being close to nature, and enjoying the moment. Since she has realized that she is not only a human being but is a citizen of the cosmos, she has been discovering more and more that she is in this life to make a difference and to add something worthy to the world.

Part of her life's mission is to spread love, peace, consciousness, and gratitude and appreciation every day, to help people to be more conscious of who they are, and to help them understand how to be happier in each moment and find their balance.

She believes that life is found in the depth of each moment.

www.ingramcontent.com/pod-product-compliance
Lightning Source LLC
Chambersburg PA
CBHW052111090426
42741CB00009B/1764